# LAW
# OF
# ATTRACTION

## Praise For Stella's Transformational Coaching Program: "Find Your Happy"

*I once saw a movie with Burt Lancaster in which he said that in order for things to remain the same, we need to change. And this is how Stella Frances helped me.*

*I learned to allow myself to choose to move forward. I changed for the better because she showed me how to dig deep into my soul and bring out the best in me.*

*I have made changes that needed to be made for quite some time, so my soul, my spirit can now progress and ultimately shine. Everyone has a purpose and we sometimes get sidetracked in life, this is what Stella does best, she is a guiding light in the darkest of times.*

*Forever grateful.*

Frank V, NY

*Finding myself completely unhappy and discontented with my current employment, I sought the coaching services of Stella Frances.*

*With her mentoring, guidance and encouragement, I was able to rediscover my personal values and career passion. Creating the confidence to pursue a position that brings me happiness with a financially abundant future.*

*Thank you!*

Lynette M, FL

# Praise For Stella's Transformational Coaching Program: "Find Your Happy"

Stella's coaching tools and method together with her vibrant personality has helped me discover my dream through my creative expression in Art and how to pursue it.

It's been an incredible journey of self-knowledge and awakened creativity towards my passion for painting and I AM LOVING IT!!! It's a new lifestyle and a new way of thinking for me!

So Grateful!!

Zetta K, FL

As my life coach I trusted Stella completely. She was very aware of my growth and gave me positive feedback when she saw I understood and was becoming more aware. She got me to think deeply about my Dream and how to attain it and made me aware of things that short-circuit its attainment.

She gave me the tools that were necessary to achieve my goals. I feel she knows me better than I know myself. She has a very cheerful and warm approach and is always joyful when she speaks to you. She truly cares about you and your success. She lives what she teaches, has a giving heart and a loving spirit.

God bless Stella.

Stuart W, CT

## Praise For Stella's Corporate Training: "Steps to Success" and "Stella Notes"

*Stella is definitely the "Queen of Happiness" and her passion to make this world a happier place is an art form, that Leonardo da Vinci would be proud of.*

*I have seen Stella speak with various audiences, and she has captivated their attention for many hours at a time. Stella speaks from the heart and soul, and her words are very inspirational in helping people get back on the road to true happiness.*

*Her **Stella Notes** series of books gives even the "no time to read" individuals, the ability to change their lives in a positive way that will bring peace even in times of despair. To know Stella is to love everything about her, and she will touch your heart with Solutions from the Soul that will make your life a better and happier one!*

John Ondrejack, P.E.
Manager-Southeast/Caribbean Region
Water Resource/Power Pump Sales
Flowserve Solutions Group

## Other STELLA NOTES BOOKS

- ❖ Law of Attraction
- ❖ Imagine
- ❖ Inspired
- ❖ Dreams Come True
- ❖ No Worries
- ❖ Being Happier
- ❖ Stuck No More
- ❖ Happy by Habit
- ❖ The Power of No
- ❖ Love Thyself
- ❖ Mindfully Yours
- ❖ Find Your Purpose

Every Month we add new titles in our Happiness Library filled with tips and tools to make your journey a Fun One! Be sure to check them out!

This book is being given to

_____

*Because I care about you and your happiness*

*With Love,*

_____

# Law of Attraction

## Harnessing Your Creative Power

# STELLA FRANCES

Happiness Coach & Success Trainer

Alpha ★ Aster Press

Copyright © 2019 by Stella Frances

All rights reserved. Printed in the United States of America.
This book or any portion thereof may not be reproduced or used in any manner whatsoever without the express written permission of the publisher except for the use of brief quotations in critical articles and reviews.
For information address: Alpha Aster Press, 103 S Us Hwy One, Ste F-5, Jupiter, FL, 33477

First Printing: 2019

ISBN 978-0-359-52917-9

Alpha★Aster Press

Cover design: ZettaKarmas.com
Photos of Stella: WoodstockStudio.com

Ordering Information: Special discounts are available on quantity purchases by corporations, associations, educators, and others. For details, contact the publisher at the above listed address.

U.S. trade bookstores and wholesalers, contact Alpha★Aster Press
sales@alphaaster.com

**This book is dedicated to:**

*My father Vasilis, who taught me the value of truth.*

*I Thank you for your love with all my heart.*
Xo

---

*Very little is needed to make a happy life;*
*it is all within yourself, in your way of thinking.*

MARCUS AURELIUS

# CONTENTS

Preface ................................................................................. iii

Introduction by Stella Frances ................................................ vii

ACT I: INFORMATIVE GUIDEBOOK .......................................... 1

    Introduction ........................................................................ 5

    « Chapter One »  What is the Law of Attracton ..................... 9

    « Chapter Two »  How To Begin............................................ 15

    « Chapter Three »  The Basics............................................... 23

    « Chapter Four »  The Examples ........................................... 29

    « Chapter Five »  The Pitfalls ................................................. 35

    « Chapter Six »  Final Thoughts............................................. 43

        Notes At A Glance ............................................................. 47

ACT II: EMPOWERING WORKBOOK........................................ 53

    « Chapter Seven » Happier Through Self-Reflection ................ 55

ACT III: KEY FACTS ................................................................. 75

    « Chapter Eight »  Building Blocks......................................... 77

ACT IV: HAPPINESS BUILDERS - TOOLS-TO-USE ..................... 91

    « Chapter Nine »  Pay It Forward........................................... 92

        Words of Wisdom ............................................................. 105

        Pearls of Kindness............................................................ 111

        Relaxing Mandalas............................................................ 117

IN CLOSING: BONUS MATERIAL: 2 Gifts For You .................... .123

AFTERWORD: Resource Guide for Living A Happier Life.......... 131

## Acknowledgments

I acknowledge with heartfelt happiness and gratitude:

My clients and students for their encouragement to spread the word about true happiness through the Stella Notes.

My participants to my seminars and presentations who have shown their support for my work and who continue to be an inspiration to me.

My mentors and teachers who shared their knowledge and wisdom with me, while they believed in my wildest dream and breakthrough goal: To spread happiness around the globe!

Everyone who makes the effort to bring a smile to the world, even on the days the sun's hiding behind the clouds.

My awesome friends, amazing family, and the best sister in the whole wide world who surround me with unconditional love, smiles, and fun times.

---

*Knowing yourself is the beginning of all wisdom.*
ARISTOTLE

---

# "I Believe We Were Born To Be Happy"
## Mentor, Coach, Speaker, Creator of Stella-Notes

Hi and thank you for checking out this publication. Stella Frances, here, founder of Elevated Awareness, on a mission to empower you.

My goal is to add more value to your world than you ever thought possible by giving you tools you can use to live a great life.

Having trained with Jack Canfield, America's #1 Success Coach and Co-Author of "Chicken Soup for the Soul", and as a certified DreamBuilder Coach, I am known to deliver innovative and high-quality personal development training with proven results that have changed many lives.

I help people like you dream big and back it up with daily actions to create measurable results. That's because I care deeply about you and I am committed to not only get you results but make learning irresistibly fun.

Through my products, seminars, and programs you'll learn practical wisdom and how to apply it to your everyday life. Through the Stella Notes, I want to encourage you and inspire you to take charge of your happiness and success by boosting your life and business skills, dropping excuses and adding massive amounts of fun into your every day.

Make the most of the Stella Notes by completing the exercises, practicing daily affirmation, and building new habits that will contribute to taking your happiness and wellbeing to the next level. Much Love, Stella Frances

# THE GREATEST GIFT: YOUR OWN PERSONAL DEVELOPMENT

The greatest gift you can give somebody is your own personal development.

I used to say, "If you will take care of me, I will take care of you."

Now I say, "I will take care of me for you, if you will take care of you for me."

—Jim Rohn

The Stella Notes is all about personal development for everyone, within the context of self-discovery & transformation. Personal development is the ongoing, lifelong process of learning, knowing and understanding who we are, why we're here and what work we have come to do in our lifetime, what our gifts and abilities are, and how to build them up, so that we can live up to our highest potential.

If you find yourself in a situation that needs to change. If you have reached a plateau wondering what's next, look at the "man/woman in the mirror" and decide to make a change by changing your ways. the *Stella Notes* gives you winning ways to successfully do so.

# CLUB ★ HAPPY

*Know thyself.*
SOCRATES

The success that followed the launching of the Stella Notes led me to the next step which was to create a loving, caring, physical or virtual space, where we get to connect, share ideas, and support each other. And so, the Club was born!

***"Club-Happy" is not your ordinary book club.*** Consider it your social group, your support group, your mastermind group, your cheerleader group. Once a week we get together in-person or on a call to connect by brainstorming new ideas, solving problems, learning from each other and growing together.

Fact of life is that we need each other to grow and evolve, especially when we decide to make a change. Our motto at the Club-Happy is simple. We come together with the aim to live better lives by finding and implementing empowering solutions to the problems we are experiencing in our personal and professional lives. The intention of Club-Happy is to help each other grow and expand by implementing the practices, tools, and strategies that are included in the Stella Notes books.

## Be Part Of An Empowering Group Of People

Having 2,000 friends on Facebook may be great but personal connections are much more powerful. Club-Happy is about building great relationships personal and professional, as we get together and connect by sharing knowledge and helping each other grow.

As a member of Club-Happy you are an important part of a conscious community that shares the same vision. The vision of attaining and maintaining true happiness. A peaceful, balanced, and harmonious way of being.

There are so many reasons why join Club-Happy. Every in-person meeting or call is well structured with clear boundaries and expectations, runs based on a mutually agreed upon agenda to help us stay on track as we share evenly.

## Why Join CLUB★ HAPPY:

1. To create deep, lasting connections with like-minded people.
2. To clear confusion and gain focus and clarity on your vision.
3. To be courageous, advantageous and spontaneous.
4. To become the person, you know you can be.
5. To create a clear vision and an action plan.
6. To socialize and be part of a fun group.
7. To think bigger and more creatively.
8. To be accountable.
9. To support others.
10. To be supported.
11. To be happier.
12. To be You.

I invite you to join me today and start enjoying the tremendous benefits of being part of Club-Happy. Visit https://stellafrances.com/clubhappy/ for more information or reach out with your questions, at Happier@StellaFrances.com

# INTRODUCTION BY STELLA FRANCES
## Suggestions To My Readers

A very warm welcome to this reading experience. My intention for creating the Stella Notes, series of practical books, is very specific. I want to help you harness your inner-power, connect with your truth, and create a life that is in harmony with your soul. And in return I promise, you will get to deep lasting happiness, for the only place to find your true happy is within you.

The Stella Notes will help you learn new ways of bringing positive change into your life in the most effective winning ways with the least amount of effort. Originally, I created the *Stella Notes,* with a specific audience in the mind of my heart. The people who have no time to read and the people who are not fans of reading. **My sister gave me the idea.** Knowledge is power, but reading is not her favorite past time.

As an artist, my sister Zetta, loves to paint. Often, I'd hear her say, *"If there was a book for non-readers, I would read it."* By that she meant, a few pages, clear language easy to read, helpful to the point useful material and of course pictures. Being an avid reader myself I didn't want her to miss out on knowledge and so here we are.

### How To Use The Stella Notes Books

The Stella Notes is a series of books structured to make reading and absorption of the material real easy. The information is presented in four sections. Each section is called **ACT**. Here's what you will find in every Stella Notes book:

- ❖ **ACT I:** Guidebook: Theory of Concept.
- ❖ **ACT II:** Workbook: Self-Reflection on the Concept.
- ❖ **ACT III:** Key Facts: Additional Information.
- ❖ **ACT IV:** Mindful and Practical Tools-to-Use.

You can read the guidebook in *ACT I* at one seating or in small bits, however it suits you. Answer the questions in the workbook as presented in *ACT II* at your pace. Here, you can write down the answers in your book or get a notebook and start jotting them down there. In *ACT III* **Key Facts** you will find additional information about the main subject.

While in *ACT IV* you will be pleasantly surprised by a beautiful collection of words of wisdom, pearls of kindness in the form of heartfelt affirmations, and magnificent mandalas to help you stay in the moment, find inner peace and express your inner-artist. The pearls of kindness are beautiful positive statements designed to help you build new empowering beliefs through repetition. The words of wisdom I bring to you, were spoken by some of the most powerful and advanced thinkers in our world. Listen to the echo of their voices and use their valuable knowledge in your moment-to-moment life.

In the Afterword section, under resources you will find tools you can use to build the above ideas and they are all totally **FREE**. This is my way of saying Thank You. *Go to the website StellaFrances.com/resources and download them there.* Use the *Gratitude Journal* to record you wins and gifts of the day. Use the *Get Unstuck Tool* for days when you feel just a tad stuck…we all go there and need this tool. Same with the *Priority Finder Tool*.

Who doesn't get stressed or overwhelmed with the complexities of our lives? The *Daily Success Habits* will help you with just that. Create new success habits. Finally, the *5-Day Grow-Expand-Thrive Mini Course* will help you exhilarate towards your new life. The life of your choice.

## Why Read The Stella Notes Books? Because You Will Learn New, Winning Ways Of Thinking...Guarantee!

The practice of planting high quality seedlings of new positive, powerful, constructive thoughts in our minds creates our ideal results. I've been practicing and experimenting this truth for the past 20 years. I know it works.

Remember this. To change your LifeStyle, you must first change your ThoughtStyle. Opening up to the thoughts of great thinkers is one sure way to get inspired and start thinking different thoughts. Makes sense? Albert Einstein defined insanity as the act of trying to solve a problem with the same thinking that created it.

At first, it may seem or even feel a little strange but stay with it. Give it time, let it flourish. You will be amazed at what you will harvest.

---

*Happiness is the meaning and the purpose of life, the whole aim and end of human existence.*
ARISTOTLE

## Are You Willing To *Believe In Yourself?*

Finally, a word of caution. As with anything worth having in life it takes time, commitment and dedication. It takes effort to create something worth having.

❖ *What's worth more than, living a life you totally love living?*

❖ *What's worth more than, being happy from within?*

❖ *What's worth more than, having found meaning in your life?*

So, go ahead dare to design your life, find meaning and live it the way you want, for you know best how to find what you're looking for. And as you do, practice self-love through kindness and forgiveness towards yourself. Be patient with you.

Be the light of love in your life. Give yourself the best love you can give yourself. <u>**BELIEVE IN YOU**</u>. **And when you do, you will be amazed as you discover who you truly are and what you can create when you release the brakes of yesterday.**

Read the Stella Notes, Solutions from the Soul, any way you like. Cover to cover, one paragraph, one quote, one affirmation at a time. Keep your book by your side, make it your constant companion. It is designed in such way that however you use it you will feel inspired to move forward from where you are.

Whether you read one page, one sentence or just run the questions you will start seeing changes and eventually results in your life. You will find yourself be more motivated, more engaged, more curious, more alive and above all happier.

*"Magically?"* You may ask.

Well, life is magical and so are you. Once you start tapping into your super powers there will be no stopping. You have in your procession an amazing tool, an extraordinary component. That is your brain. And you are given unlimited potential. Put them to work with the information I will be sharing with you through the Stella Notes books and you will be well on your way to creating pure and lasting happiness and unstoppably so.

You are brave. Choose to leave behind the voice of fear and doubt and you will be amazed at what you will create. Courage is not the absence of fear. Courage is facing fear.

The Stella Notes books bring you unique concepts that focus on mindset, contribute to your personal growth, and provide you with tools you can use and strategies to implement that will help you change your thoughts and therefore your world.

Let's begin!

With Love and Gratitude,
XO Stella

P.S. If you know it's time to bring radical change into your life and need support, reach out and contact me through the website. I am here to help.

# ACT I:

## INFORMATIVE GUIDEBOOK

knowledge:
the pathway to
happiness & success

# A man is but the product of his thoughts what he thinks, he becomes.
## Mahatma Gandhi

## Love: The One Creative Force

A college professor had his sociology class go into the Baltimore slums to get case histories of 200 young boys. They were asked to write an evaluation of each boy's future.

In every case the students wrote, *"He hasn't got a chance."*

Twenty-five years later another sociology professor came across the earlier study. He had his students follow up on the project to see what had happened to these boys.

With the exception of 20 boys who had moved away or died, the students learned that 176 of the remaining 180 had achieved more than ordinary success as lawyers, doctors and businessmen.

The professor was astounded and decided to pursue the matter further. Fortunately, all the men were in the area and he was able to ask each one, *"How do you account for your success?"* In each case the reply came with feeling, *'There was a teacher."*

The teacher was still alive, so he sought her out and asked the old but still alert lady what magic formula she had used to pull these boys out of the slums into successful achievement.

The teacher's eyes sparkled, and her lips broke into a gentle smile. *"It's really very simple,"* she said. *"I loved those boys."*

Chicken Soup for the Soul,

(Canfield, 1993)

> *"Spread love everywhere you go: first of all, in your own house. Give love to your children, to your wife or husband, to a next-door neighbor. Let no one ever come to you without leaving better and happier. Be the living expression of God's kindness; kindness in your face, kindness in your eyes, kindness in your smile, kindness in your warm greeting."*
>
> MOTHER TERESA

# Law of Attraction

## Harnessing Your Creative Power

## Introduction

You may have heard people refer to something known as the Law of Attraction, *LOA for short*. Maybe you think it's reserved for those who are on the dating scene. Another possibility is it's a physics term dealing with particles and how they attract (or repel) each other, etc. The truth is, it is something more fundamental than both of these.

The Law of Attraction is a term that describes what many refer to as "like attracts like." The idea is what you put out into the universe you can expect to get out of it. Others will use the phrase, "what goes around comes around."

This is a primary reason why negative people are not happy, all things being equal. They put on negative vibes out into the universe, and they get them back.

Contrast this with positive people and you will see quite a difference. The positive people always seem to have things go their way. If something doesn't work out, they don't complain about it. They simply look for a better way.

Public awareness of the Law of Attraction has been around for a while. Maybe you first came across it through Napoleon Hill and his book "Think and Grow Rich", or maybe you first heard about it when the book and movie "The Secret" became popular and were discussed everywhere, including the Oprah Show. No matter how you first came across it, or even if this is a new concept to you, this book is for you.

In the following pages and chapters, you'll find a great **introduction to the topic** along with some **thinking strategies** and **hands-on tips** for making the Law Of Attraction work in your favor. The basic idea is that "like attracts like".

This means **you can improve your life in any area you may choose.** Whether it is your circumstances, your finances, your relationships, your weight, or something else. *Any aspect of your life can be changed in a positive way by actively thinking and visualizing your IDEAL outcome.* Does that mean you can meditate about getting a million dollars and the money will fall magically in your lap? Of course not. There's a lot more to this idea and quite a bit of science to back it up.

*Curious?* Keep on reading to learn more about the Law of Attraction. We'll start with an introductory chapter about what the Law of Attraction is and what is not. I have some facts and science to share with you and show you the **Law of Attraction is a natural universal law of life** that works just as reliably as gravity does.

Next, we take a look at how you can make the Law of Attraction work for you and start actively incorporating it's power into your everyday life. We'll talk about defining goals and what we need to do to get closer to them and reach them.

**I will share with you my notes of what helped me successfully create radical change in my life.** And I am confident this information will make it easier for you to understand the Law of Attraction and produce results in your favor. **It will also help you practice positive thinking until it becomes a well-engrained habit.**

To solidify what you are learning and to better understand how the Law of Attraction works we'll go over some real-life examples before wrapping things up with a chapter on common pitfalls and how to avoid them.

There is no limit to what the law can do for you. Dare to believe in your own IDEAL; think of the IDEAL as an already accomplished fact.
Charles F. Haanel

## « Chapter One »

## WHAT IS THE LAW OF ATTRACTION?

THE LAW OF ATTRACTION is a natural law like the law of gravity for example. The big difference is that it is slightly more difficult to quantify and measure. With the law of gravity, you can drop a ball and observe it fall to the ground. You can weigh the ball, measure the height, time the fall, and come up with a formula.

Law of Attraction is a little harder to measure and prove, and while it is easy to observe, it's much harder to quantify precisely. This is one of the main reasons it has not yet been adopted by most scientists. As you'll discover shortly, the more we learn about the molecular makeup of our world and quantum physics, the closer we come to an idea of our world that aligns with the concept of the Law of Attraction.

This basic concept is that everything is made of energy and that our thoughts and feelings influence the world around us. The Law of Attraction states that "like attracts like" and that thoughts attract corresponding situations and circumstances.

Another way to express this is to say that whatever you give attention to is what shows up in reality. In other words, by focusing our thinking, we can change the circumstances and our perception of the opportunities around us in a way that helps us reach our goals.

On the flip side, if we're not careful about our thoughts and what we pay attention to, we can attract a lot of negative things into our lives.

I know this sounds very "New Age" and the whole idea of thinking yourself into a more successful, healthier, and happier person may seem strange. Yet, I bet you've experienced this yourself already.

Think back on a time when you were thinking about getting a new car. You look at some options and fall in love with a Honda Fit. All of sudden, you see Honda Fit everywhere. You see them driving around, in parking lots and spot them for sale on car lots and in the local paper.

Did your thinking create dozens of new cars that are now driving around in your town?

Of course not, instead your perception has changed and with that your circumstances have adjusted and you're seeing this particular model car everywhere.

Let's look at one more quick example you may be familiar with. Let's say you order something online and it is not what you expected. You call up customer service. You have two options. You can get mad and angry at the company and thus the customer service person, yell, and throw a fit.

Or you can be pleasant, explain what happened, and ask what they can do to fix it. In the first scenario you're focusing on the bad and negative. In the second, you're thinking about finding a solution and a positive outcome.

In which scenario do you think the customer service rep is more likely to make things right for you, and go out of their way to make you happy?

Why is it that we feed off each other's emotions, start to pay attention to the things we focus on, and attract the things we think about into our lives? A concept that explains this phenomenon perfectly is the Law of Vibration.

According to this law everything is in motion. We start to see it under the microscope as we are able to magnify further and further. On a molecular level, we are not one solid body. Instead we are little bits of energy that spin around each other in a very precise and organized manner.

Everything in our world on an atomic level is in constant motion. With that motion, everything gives off vibrations and we can use our minds to change those vibrations to match those of the things and people we want to attract into our lives. It's a matter of dialing into the frequency for the life we want.

If you put yourself into a mindset that the company you ordered from will set things right for you, you're transmitting a vibration that encourages positivity and cooperation. The customer service person on the other end receives that vibration and will gladly offer you an exchange for something that better represents what you wanted.

Now that you have a better understanding of the Law of Attraction, what it is, how it works, and how the law of vibration comes into play, let's look at what you can do to change your habits and your ways of thinking to use the Law of Attraction in your life.

# Nothing can prevent your picture from coming into concrete form except the same power which gave it birth -Yourself.
Genevieve Berhrend

14 STELLA FRANCES

## « Chapter Two »

## HOW TO BEGIN USING THE LAW OF ATTRACTION IN YOUR LIFE

**N**ow that you have a pretty good overview of what the Law of Attraction is, it's time to talk about how you can make it work for you. It's all good and well to talk about "like attracts like" and that we need to send out the right vibrations to get what we want, but how do you actually make it work?

Implementing the Law of Attraction is all about changing your mind – both the conscious and the subconscious. I'm going to walk you through a simple, four-step process that will help you implement what you've learned so far.

Ready to improve your life and attract the things and people to help you do just that? Here's what you do…

## Decide What You Want in Life

The first step **to getting what you want in life** is to decide what exactly you want. It makes sense, right? If you don't know where you're going it's hard to plot a course. Think of this part as figuring out your destination. It's hard to use a map and get to where you want to go unless you have a firm grasp of where you're going.

Think about the 4 main aspects of your life. See the list below. What requires of your immediate attention? What areas of your life would you like to improve? Decide what you want to change and employ the courage, commitment, and attitude that will take you there.

---

**THE 4 MAIN ASPECTS OF LIFE**

1. **Health.** *Wellbeing, Fit and Trim, Ideal Weight*
2. **Love.** *Relationships with the Self, with Others*
3. **Business, Career**
4. **Time and Money Freedom**

---

Pick what stands out for you from the above list. Come up with one or two areas of your life you'd like to improve.

Focus on what's most important for you right now and tackle it first.

If you're new to the idea of the Law Of Attraction and things like visualization and attracting what you want into your life, I recommend you pick one specific area, set one goal and work towards achieving it.

**HINT: Be specific.** Don't just decide that you want to lose weight. It's hard to visualize something unless you become very clear about what you want. Instead, a much better goal would be to lose 50 pounds and fit into a size 6 pair of jeans for example.

## Write It Down

Once you know what you want in your life, get out a notebook and a pen and write it down. Write a description of what you want to attract. A great way of doing this is to write it in the present tense. Instead of writing down what you want your life to be, describe it as if you already have the life you want. Instead of writing down what it will be like when you lose that extra weight, or get out of credit card debt, write it down as if you are already living that life. Here are two examples:

- ❖ *My IDEAL weight is* 130lb. I feel great in my *size 6* jeans. I am happy and grateful I am wearing more form fitted clothes.
- ❖ *I fall asleep easily* at night, knowing that my family is financially secure.

Be as detailed and descriptive as you can when you write down what your life will be like once you attract the things you desire. The more detailed you can be during this process the better.

Write about how easy it is to get out of bed in the morning now that your back is no longer bothering you, or the delicious, healthy food you enjoy as part of your healthy slim lifestyle.

Spend as much time as you need to write this down. Use a pen and paper to connect on a deeper level with this material. What you're creating is a vision of what your future life will be. Paint a vivid picture with words of what your goals in life are. Speaking of visualization...

## Visualize

Next, it's time to start visualizing what it will be like when you change your life and reach your goals. You've made a good start when you were writing things down. The key now is to get in the habit of recreating that image and visualizing it in great detail as often as possible.

Remember when we were talking about the law of vibration and how in the Law Of Attraction like attracts like? By visualizing you put yourself on the right frequency to attract the opportunities and people in your life that will help you make it happen.

It also gets you into a mental space of making decisions on a daily basis that will help you move closer and closer to your goal. No, visualizing a much slimmer and fitter version of yourself will not magically melt off the extra pounds. What it will do is help you make better choices when it comes to food.

That apple on the counter will start to look a lot tastier than that Twinkie in the cupboard. You'll feel more energized and be ready to head out for a walk when a friend calls to see if you want to join her.

Spend some time right now visualizing yourself having reached the results you're looking for. Sit down in a comfortable chair, close your eyes, and put yourself in that space. Be as detailed as possible. What do you look like, what are you wearing, what are your settings? What does it smell like, what does it feel like? Create a very detailed vision of the new and improved version of yourself.

As your mind starts to wander, bring it back to the vision. Focus on it and make it real in your head. It takes some concentration and don't be surprised if you can't "hold" your vision very long in the beginning. Keep practicing and it will get easier. The more you visualize and the more vividly you do it, the faster you'll see results. I have also included some tips and ideas to help you with this in the next chapter.

## Create A Ritual

The more you practice the visualization we talked about, the better you'll get at it and the sooner you'll reach your goals and build the life you want. As with anything else, it takes time and effort to get into the habit of visualizing regularly. The best way to make sure that happens is to create a daily ritual for yourself.

Find a time and place that's convenient and conducive to your visualization exercises. Pick a comfortable spot and a place and time when you likely won't be interrupted. Start going through your visualization exercise each day and turn it into a daily ritual. It won't take you long before it becomes a habit. As you work through your "visualization ritual" focus on seeing, feeling, and experiencing your desired results.

One tip to make this easier is to attach this new Law of Attraction ritual to an existing ritual. For example, if you're already starting your day by pouring a cup of coffee and then quietly sitting by the kitchen window to drink it, you can make this new practice part of that morning ritual. Instead of starting from scratch, you're adding to it, making it easier for you to make it part of your daily routine.

Once you have your ritual established, do everything you can to make sure you go through it daily. Don't start changing things around until you have it firmly established and it becomes an automatic habit like brushing your teeth before you go to bed.

This simple little exercise will ensure that you get and stay tuned to the vibration to attract those new positive things into your life.

# ACTION NOTES

## ACTION NOTES

### THE 4-STEP PROCESS

1. DECIDE WHAT YOU WANT
2. WRITE IT DOWN
3. VISUALIZE IT
4. CREATE A RITUAL

Take action today. Follow the above steps and start creating your IDEAL outcome.

# Everyone visualizes whether he knows it or not. Visualizing is the great secret of success.
Genevieve Berhrend

## « Chapter Three »

### TIPS TO HELP YOU IMPLEMENT THE LAW OF ATTRACTION

**C**REATING A HABIT OF visualizing daily and making it a ritual is great, but there is more you can do to implement the Law Of Attraction. Remember the more strongly you create the reality you want to see in your life inside your mind, the quicker your own frequency changes and you start to make things happen. With that in mind (pun intended), here are a few extra tips to help you implement this. Put them to use as much and as often as possible.

I encourage you to give all of these a try. Get a feel for what works best for you. Ideally, you want to use all of them on a regular basis, but at the very least incorporate the ones that resonate with you the most on a daily basis.

Think of it as workouts for your brain. You want to train your brain to focus on your desired life results.

# TIP #1:
# Create Vision Boards

One of my favorite tools is the vision board. It's a physical reminder of your intentions. Not only will you get a firm grasp on your visualization as you work on your vision board, every time you glance at it, you'll be taken back to that moment and it will strengthen your intentions.

Get out a poster board, find that box of markers, and start looking for visual representations of what you want to manifest. You can divide your vision board up into different sections that represent the different areas of your life that you want to improve. A quick Google search for vision boards will give you plenty of ideas and inspiration. Print images out, cut them out of magazines and catalogs, and don't forget to write down your intentions and affirmations as well.

There is no right or wrong way to create a vision board. Grab your scissors and glue stick and get started.

## TIP #2
## Practice Meditation and Incorporate Visualization

Visualizing what you want your life to be can be hard. It takes practice and patience with yourself. Your daily visualization ritual will help you get better at this. Something else that's very beneficial is meditation. It works the same "mental muscles" and helps you get better at envisioning what you want and getting on the right frequency. Start with guided meditation and then move into a form that incorporates your visualization.

## TIP #3
## Write And Memorize Affirmations

Another great way to make sure your intentions are in line with what you want in life is to write and memorize affirmations that you can then repeat throughout the day.

The key here is to write affirmations that will be helpful, not harmful. Always write them in the present tense as if what you want in life is already here. It is also helpful to not create an affirmation that you don't completely believe is attainable or makes you focus on how far you have to go.

For example, instead of writing something along the lines of "I have lost 75 pounds and am slim and trim" (which keeps reminding you about just how overweight you are), come up with an affirmation like "I am feeling more comfortable in my skin and can move with ease. My pants keep getting looser and looser".

# TIP #4
# Most Importantly - Take Action

Last but not least, let's talk about taking action. This is the most important step in making the Law of Attraction work. One of the biggest misconceptions about the Law of Attraction is that you simply think about something and it magically falls into your lap. This is not how it works.

By focusing on what you want and using the Law of Attraction, you will become more "in tune" with your goals and desires. Law of Attraction may bring you the ideas, chance meetings with people who can help you, or any other kind of opportunity. But without action, nothing is going to happen.

## ACT Today. ACT Now!

You must constantly move in the direction of your goals if you want to create the results you desire. For example, if you're looking to get out of debt and a business acquaintance offers you a side project to make extra cash, say yes and get to work.

If you're trying to lose weight and get into better shape and a friend calls you up and invites you to go out for a walk, do it.

If you want to live in a beautiful home with lots of light and space, start cleaning up the place you live in now. Declutter. Give it a fresh coat of paint and do what you can right now to align it more with your vision of your dream home.

# STRATEGY NOTES

> ## STRATEGY NOTES
>
> ## BUILD NEW HABITS
>
> 1. Create Vision Boards
> 2. Practice Meditation
> 3. Incorporate Visualization
> 4. Write And Memorize Affirmations
> 5. Take Action

You have taken action and you decided what your IDEAL outcome would be. Now use the tools to set your winning strategy that will support you to turn your Ideal from idea to reality.

**TOOLS TO USE:** Vison Board, Meditation, Visualization, Affirmations, Action!

## « Chapter Four »

## EVERY DAY EXAMPLES SHOWING THE LAW OF ATTRACTION IN ACTION

**I HAVE SHARED EXAMPLES** of what the Law of Attraction can do throughout this book. To drive the point home and help you realize what can happen when you put your mind to it and set your intentions, let's run through a few more examples that touch different areas and aspects of our lives.

In each example, I show you one possible way that the Law of Attraction may manifest a goal. I hope this will help you spot opportunities and notice when your own positive thinking is working and the universe is showing you a path towards your dreams and desires.

# EXAMPLE #1
# When You're Looking For A New Job

You've set your intentions on finding a new job. Out of the blue, a friend mentions a new company they heard was looking for help. The job description may not align perfectly with what you had in mind, but once you start to talk to the owner, you learn that he is looking for someone with your exact qualifications.

# EXAMPLE #2
# When you're Searching For Ways To Grow Your Business

Let's say you're working on your online business and you're asking the universe to help you grow. You're on social media sharing blog posts and see an ad about growing your list through Facebook advertising. You may not have considered paying for traffic or leads, but this may be just the thing that helps you get to the next level.

## EXAMPLE #3
## Losing Weight And Getting In Shape For Your Grandkids

You're tired of being overweight and want to lose a few pounds so you can keep up with the grandchildren at the park. A friend calls you up and asks you to join the new walking club they have just joined. Say yes, take action and it may just turn out that your friend has similar goals and the two of you can help each other and hold each other accountable.

## EXAMPLE #4
## Wanting To Retire Early

Your dream is to retire in your early 50s with plenty of money set aside, so you can travel and do all the things you want to do after you stop working. You have a financial plan in place but you are about $50,000 short of reaching your goal. It's hard to set aside money for retirement while also saving up for your child's college fund.

While applying to university, your child is given information about scholarship opportunities. You look into it, spend a lot of time finding and applying for various scholarships and grants. As a result your child's college education is almost completely paid for. You encourage her to get a part time job to pay for room and board. The end result? Your child gets a great education, learns important life skills at the part time job and you get to retire early.

# EXAMPLE #5
## Fitting More Travel Into Your Busy Life

You want to travel more, but your busy job doesn't allow you to take more than two weeks off per year. It's putting a serious damper on your travel schedule. Using the Law of Attraction you set the intention to have more travel opportunities. A few weeks later your company offers you a sales position that will have you travel all around the world. Yes, you'll be working, but there will also be plenty of opportunities to visit and sightsee, plus you get to meet locals and experience work life in different cultures.

What I want you to take away from these examples is this: the Law of Attraction works, but it doesn't always work in the way you expect it to. Your job, after getting very clear about what you want and aligning your mind with it, is to keep your eyes and mind open to the opportunities that will present themselves.

33 THE LAW OF **ATTRACTION**

Everything you want is out there waiting for you to ask. Everything you want also wants you, but you have to take action to get it.
Jack Canfield

34 STELLA FRANCES

## « Chapter Five »

## PITFALLS TO AVOID WHEN IMPLEMENTING THE LAW OF ATTRACTION

**THE BASIC CONCEPT** of the Law of Attraction is fairly simple. Get clear about what you want in life and ask for it. If it's so simple and easy, why don't we all get exactly what we want then? And why isn't everyone practicing the Law Of Attraction techniques on a regular basis? The problem is that there are some things you may be doing unintentionally to sabotage yourself. Let's look at these common pitfalls and more importantly what you can do to avoid them.

# PITFALL #1
# You're Missing An Emotional Connection With Your Intentions

When we first started talking about the Law of Attraction in chapter one, I mentioned the law of vibration and that we have to align ourselves with the right intentions. In other words, we have to give off the right frequency to attract the things we want into our lives.

The other part to that story is that we need to make sure those intentions vibrate strongly enough to make sure they carry and are effective. That's where our emotional connection with our intentions comes into play. Think of it as a way to charge or even supercharge those vibrations.

Without an emotional connection and investment into your intention, little will happen. Get enthusiastic about the changes you want in your life and you'll see progress much sooner.

You have to really want something and be passionate about that change to change your vibrations. Don't hold back. Invest emotionally in your desired life and become passionate about the things you want to attract.

# PITFALL #2
# Do you Believe You Can Change?

For the Law of Attraction to work, you have to believe that you or your circumstances can change. You have to believe it 100%. That's why visualization exercises can work extremely well. When you visualize you put yourself into that space. You are the wealthy, confident, slim person with the great house and you believe that you deserve every bit of it.

If you're having trouble with the "believing 100%" part, start smaller. You may not yet believe that you can lose 50 pounds, but you know without a shadow of a doubt that you can lose 5.

Start there and work your way up. As you start to believe that you can make bigger and bigger leaps, you'll start to make progress more quickly.

## PITFALL #3
## You're Missing Opportunities That Present Themselves

When you look back through the examples of the Law Of Attraction in action in the last chapter, you may have noticed that one of the interesting things is that things don't always work the way you expect them too.

If you're closed minded or set on a particular path, you may miss a lot of great opportunities that present themselves to you. Learn to say yes more, and step outside of your comfort zone. The changes you are looking for may be just around the corner, but along a path you have not yet considered.

# PITFALL #4
# Your Affirmations Are Working Against You

Affirmations are a great tool to help you align your mind, conscious, and subconscious with the things you want to achieve. They can also work against you when used incorrectly.

Make sure you create affirmations that help you stay in a positive frame of mind. Here's an example of what I mean. Let's say you want to attract more wealth into your life. An affirmation of "I am wealthy and have plenty of money to spend" may not be your best choice when this simple sentence constantly reminds you of how tight finances may be right now. Pay attention to how you react to your affirmation and make sure you choose wisely. Choose statements that help you get into the right frame of mind and are not reminders of the things you don't want.

A better example in this case might be: "Every day, more and more opportunities to create wealth present themselves to me and I take advantage of each one."

# PITFALL #5
# You're Not Taking Action

The most important component to making the Law of Attraction work for you is to take action. You may have heard the saying "Act As If". Start acting as if you are already living your ideal life today.

The worst thing you can do is to do nothing and wait for your dream life to fall into place for you. It's not going to happen. If you want to be fit and slim, start moving more and make smart food choices each day. If you want to find Mr. or Mrs. Right, go out there and meet new people. Be open to new relationships until you find the right person. Plenty of opportunities will present themselves, you just have to take action.

While these aren't the only pitfalls or the only reasons why the Law of Attraction may not work for you, or at least not work as fast as you'd like it to work, they are the big ones. Start with this list and make sure you are avoiding all of them.

Realize that sometimes things take time to manifest, and sometimes it takes a while before you are ready to receive. Keep working on your affirmations and visualizations until you're living the life you want. Above all believe it is possible.

# ALERT NOTES

**ALERT NOTES**

1. Are you Missing An Emotional Connection With Your Intentions?

2. Do You Believe You Can Change?

3. Are you Missing Opportunities?

4. Are Your Affirmations Working Against You?

5. Are you Not Taking Action?

# The best way to overcome undesirable or negative thoughts and feelings is to cultivate the positive ones.
William Walker Atkinson

42 STELLA FRANCES

## « Chapter Six »

### FINAL THOUGHTS

**I HOPE YOU'VE ENJOYED** reading this introductory conversation about the Law of Attraction. If you're new to these concepts, I encourage you to keep an open mind and give it a try.

While this is not a full study program about every aspect of the Law of Attraction, it is a powerful introduction with actionable advice you can begin using immediately. We have covered some of the main ideas behind the Law of Attraction and I've shared plenty of tips with you that you can try and put into action right away. Let's quickly recap what we covered here.

We started with a brief introduction and definition of the Law of Attraction. We also discussed the law of vibration and how it directly relates to the Law of Attraction. This whole idea may seem a little "new age" and maybe even hokey at first glance, but I hope I have convinced you that there's a lot of science and substance to this. At the very least I hope you keep an open mind and give it a try.

In the second chapter, we discussed simple ways of implementing the Law of Attraction in your life and make it work for you. I went over a four-step process with you that involved:

- ✓ Deciding what you want in life.
- ✓ Writing it down.
- ✓ Visualizing what you want.
- ✓ Creating a ritual to make visualization a habit.

For more details refer back to chapter two. Keep working your way through these four steps and keep practicing until you have them mastered.

In chapter three I shared tips with you to help you implement these steps including creating vision boards, practicing meditation, writing down affirmations, and of course taking action.

To help illustrate how the Law of Attraction works, we went over a few everyday examples in chapter four, before moving on to common pitfalls you need to avoid in chapter five.

If you are in doubt about whether the Law of Attraction works, consider this: what do you have to lose? You give it a try, and if it doesn't seem to pan out the way you had hoped, nothing lost.

However, don't just try it once and throw in the towel. It's more of a transformative process. You need to continue until you see results.

# A man can only rise, conquer, and achieve by lifting up his thoughts.
### James Allen

# NOTES AT A GLANCE

bite size, useful practical information you can put to work for you right-away

# NOTES AT A GLANCE:
# Law of Attraction
# The Basics #1

### 1. What Is The Law Of Attraction

- ✓ Everything is made of energy and that our thoughts and feelings influence the world around us.

- ✓ The law of attraction states that "like attracts like".

- ✓ Our thoughts attract corresponding situations and circumstances.

- ✓ Whatever you give attention to is what shows up in reality.

- ✓ By focusing our thinking, we can change the circumstances and our perception of the opportunities around us.

- ✓ If we're not careful about our thoughts and what we pay attention to, we can attract a lot of negative things into our lives.

# NOTES AT A GLANCE:
# Law of Attraction
# --The Basics #2

### 2. How To Begin Using The Law Of Attraction In Your Life

- ✓ Decide what you want in life.
- ✓ Think about what you want to improve in your current life.
- ✓ Write it down. Write your goals clearly and specifically
- ✓ Visualize. Clearly picture yourself achieving your goals.
- ✓ Make it a ritual. The key is to practice visualization regularly. Try to make it just another part of your daily routine.

# NOTES AT A GLANCE:
## Law of Attraction
## --The Basics #3

### 3. Tips To Help You Implement The Law Of Attraction

- ✓ Create a vision board. Collect images of everything you want to achieve and paste/post/pin them to a board. Keep this board somewhere in plain site.

- ✓ Practice meditation. It works the same "mental muscles" as visualization and helps you get better at envisioning what you want.

- ✓ Write, memorize and use positive affirmations.

- ✓ Take action - all the "wanting" and "desire" in the world won't help you without planned thoughtful action.

# NOTES AT A GLANCE:
## Law of Attraction
## --The Basics #4

### 4. Pitfalls To Avoid When Implementing The Law Of Attraction

- ✓ Make sure you have a true emotional connection with your desires.

- ✓ Make sure you truly believe you can change.

- ✓ Don't get so lost in dreaming of the future, that you miss the opportunities of the present.

- ✓ Avoid affirmations that make you feel worse about yourself.

- ✓ Don't avoid TAKING ACTION!

Always aim at complete harmony of thought and word and deed. Always aim at purifying your thoughts and everything will be well.
Mahatma Gandhi

# ACT II:

## EMPOWERING WORKBOOK

invite more happiness into your life through the practice of self-reflection

The world as we have created it is a process of our thinking. It cannot be changed without changing our thinking.
Albert Einstein

## « Chapter Seven »

### SELF-EMPOWERMENT WORKBOOK

**You can either** read the ACTI guidebook in its entirety and then come back to the workbook, working through the section and refer back to the guide for more information as needed. Or if you prefer, you can read a chapter of the guide, and then work through the corresponding pages in this workbook. Either method works. Choose the one that works best for you and your style of learning.

Work through the material at your own pace. There is no right or wrong way to start making the Law of Attraction work for you. Take your time and really think about what you want in your life. It's important to write things down.

Not only will it help you get very clear about what you want, it also helps deepen your connection with it and gets you well on your way towards manifesting the things you want. It's also nice to be able to look back a few weeks or months from now and notice how much of what you've wanted to change in your life has already changed for the better.

As you read through the ACTI: Guidebook, you'll learn that you have to change your mind at a conscious and subconscious level to change the vibrations you're giving off.

Writing will help you get there sooner. Ideally, grab a pen, get comfortable, turn your phone off, and start working through the short exercises of this workbook. Run out of space? Use extra paper and express yourself. You don't have to work through in one sitting. Take your time, reflect on what you want to accomplish, write it down, and then come back when you're ready to work on the next section.

Let your soul be your guide.

# 1. UNDERSTANDING THE LAW OF ATTRACTION

[From: Chapter One - Page 9]

Start by reading through chapter one of the ACTI: Guide. In your own words, describe or summarize the following two concepts.

## Exercise #1.1

**What is the Law of Attraction and how does it work?**

_____
_____
_____
_____

**What is the Law of Vibration and how does it relate to the Law of Attraction?**

_____
_____
_____
_____

As you work through the exercises in the rest of this workbook it is important to have an open mind and believe in the Law of Attraction.

If you have a little voice in the back of your head telling you that this won't work, you can't get into the right mindset to change your vibration and attract the things you want into your life. Let's address this issue now with a little exercise.

*What do you think of the concept of the Law of Attraction overall?*

_____

_____

_____

*What objections do you have to this whole concept?*

_____

_____

_____

*Can you think of a few examples of where you've seen the Law of Attraction work? Read through Chapter Four of the main guide for ideas and inspiration.*

_____

_____

_____

*Are you ready to give this a serious try and overcome your objections?*

_____

_____

_____

# 2. START IMPLEMENTING THE LAW OF ATTRACTION

*[From: Chapter Two – Page 15]*

Implementing the Law of Attraction is all about changing your mind – both the conscious and the subconscious. I'm going to walk you through a simple, four-step process that will help you become very clear about what you want.

### Exercise #2.1: Decide What You Want in Life

The first step to getting what you want in life is to decide what exactly you want. Think about all aspects of your life that you could improve. This include things like:

---

**THE 4 MAIN ASPECTS OF LIFE**

1. **Health.** *Wellbeing, Fit and Trim, Ideal Weight*
2. **Love.** *Relationships with the Self, with Others*
3. **Business, Career**
4. **Time and Money Freedom**

---

Decide what you want to change and improve in all areas of your life. You can work on all of these different things, or you can focus on the most important one first, and then add the others in the mix as you get more comfortable with the next few steps.

## Time To Get Specific

Write down exactly what you want to improve or change in your life. Refer to the guide for tips on getting very clear about what you want.

## Exercise #2.2: Write It Down

Create a written account of what your life will be like when you achieve what you want in life. Take your time and be as specific and detailed as possible. Write the description in present tense and see yourself in it.

_____
_____
_____
_____
_____
_____
_____
_____
_____
_____
_____
_____
_____
_____

## Exercise #2.3: Visualize

Next, it's time to start visualizing what it will be like when you change your life and reach your goals. You've made a good start when you were writing things down. The key now is to get in the habit of recreating those images and visualizing it in great detail as often as possible.

Get comfortable, close your eyes and spend a few minutes visualizing your future life, starting with the description you wrote in the previous section.

Time for reflection.

**How did it feel to do a visualization exercise? Did it come easy, or did you have a hard time holding on to your vision?**

_____
_____
_____
_____

**How hard was it? Did you have trouble concentrating and focusing on it for more than a few minutes?**

_____
_____
_____
_____

## Exercise #2.4: Create A Ritual

The more you practice the visualization we talked about, the better you'll get at it and the sooner you'll reach your goals and build the life you want. As with anything else, it takes time and effort to get into the habit of visualizing regularly. The best way to make sure that happens is to create a daily ritual for yourself.

**When will you practice your visualization?**

_____
_____
_____
_____

**Where will you practice?**

_____
_____
_____
_____

**Are you noticing that it is getting easier?**

_____
_____
_____
_____

# 3. STRENGTHEN YOUR VISION

### [From: Chapter Three - Page 23]

Creating a habit of visualizing daily and making it a ritual is great, but there are more steps you can take to implement the Law Of Attraction.

Remember the more strongly you create the reality you want to see in your life inside your mind, the quicker your own frequency changes and you start to make things happen.

## Exercise #3.1: Create Vision Boards

Vision Boards are physical reminders of your intentions. Not only will you get a firm grasp on your visualization as you work on your vision board, every time you glance at it, you'll be taken back to that moment and it will strengthen your intentions.

1. Decide what areas of your life you want to feature on your vision board. Map it out.

2. Start gathering supplies. Where can you find visual representations of what you want to feature?

3. Create your vision board and feature it in quite a prominent place in your home or office.

# Exercise #3.2: Practice Meditation and Incorporate Visualization

Visualizing what you want your life to be can be hard. It takes practice and patience with yourself. Start making a habit of meditating daily and incorporating your visualization exercises.

**Are you familiar with meditation?**

_____
_____
_____
_____

**When and how will you start meditating?**

_____
_____
_____
_____

**What can you do to make meditation and visualization part of your daily routine?**

_____
_____
_____
_____

# Exercise #3.3: Write And Memorize Affirmations

Another great way to make sure your intentions are in line with what you want in life is to write and memorize affirmations that you can then repeat throughout the day. In the space below write three to five affirmations that you will use to solidify your vision over the coming days and weeks.

# ONE

_____
_____

# TWO

_____
_____

# THREE

_____
_____

# FOUR

_____
_____

# FIVE

_____
_____

## Exercise #3.4: Take Action

Last but not least, let's talk about taking action. This is the most important step in making the Law of Attraction work.

**What are 10 things that you can do starting right now that will help you get closer to where you want to be?**

| |
|---|
| 1. |
| 2. |
| 3. |
| 4. |
| 5. |
| 6. |
| 7. |
| 8. |
| 9. |
| 10. |

# 4. EXPLORING & AVOIDING PITFALLS

*[From: Chapter Five – Page 35]*

Let's say you've been following along, doing everything outlined in the main guide and this workbook, but you're not seeing any changes or positive results. There's a chance that you're unintentionally sabotaging yourself.

Read through chapter five about avoiding potential pitfalls in the main guide. Then come back and work through this section.

### Exercise #4.1: You're Missing An Emotional Connection With Your Intentions

You have to really want something and be passionate about that change to change your vibrations. Don't hold back. Invest emotionally in your life and become passionate about the things you want to attract.

**Do you have a strong emotional connection with your intentions?**

_____

_____

_____

**If not, spend some time reflecting on this today. Dig deep and find out why you really want to change.**

_____

_____

_____

## Exercise #4.2: Do You Believe You Can Change?

For the Law of Attraction to work, you have to believe that you or your circumstances can change.

**Look back at the changes you wrote down earlier in this workbook. Do you truly believe you can reach your goals?**

_____
_____
_____

**If not, how can you rework them to make sure it is something that you believe you can do 100%?**

_____
_____
_____

69 THE LAW OF **ATTRACTION**

# If you're interested, you will do what is convenient; if you're committed, you'll do whatever it takes.

John Assaraf

## Exercise #4.3: You're Missing Opportunities That Present Themselves

We all have a path in mind on how we will get from point A to point B. It's normal, but sometimes we get too stuck on that one path to see the opportunities around us.

**Think back over the past days and weeks. What opportunities did you miss?**

_____
_____
_____

**What can you do going forward to keep more of an open mind and take advantage of these opportunities?**

_____
_____
_____

# Exercise #4.4: Your Affirmations Are Working Against You

Affirmations are a great tool to help you align your mind, conscious, and subconscious with the things you want to achieve. They can also work against you when used incorrectly.

Take some time today to review your affirmations.

**What's working well, and what isn't?**

_____
_____
_____

**Rewrite your affirmations as needed.**

_____
_____
_____

## Exercise #4.5: You're Not Taking Action

The most important component to making the Law of Attraction work for you is to take action. Live like the life you want, starting today.

**Have you been taking action as often as you should?**

_____
_____
_____

**Have you missed opportunities because you didn't take action? List them here.**

_____
_____
_____

**What are three things you can do today to get you moving forward?**

_____
_____
_____

## 5. RECORD YOUR RESULTS

The Law of Attraction can work in "sneaky" ways. Since the opportunities that present themselves to us often don't align with what we expected, it's not uncommon that our lives change in a positive way and we don't even notice it until we take the time to reflect.

Use the space below to journal and record the progress you're making. Every week take a few minutes to reflect on what has changed and record your results below. You'll be pleasantly surprised how much progress you're making and how much your life is changing for the better.

### Week #1 Reflections

_____
_____
_____
_____

### Week #2 Reflections

_____
_____
_____
_____

## Week #3 Reflections

_____
_____
_____
_____

## Week #4 Reflections

_____
_____
_____
_____

## Week #5 Reflections

_____
_____
_____
_____

# ACT III:

## KEY FACTS

# All power is from within and therefor under our control.
### Robert Collier

## « Chapter Eight »

## BUILDING BLOCKS

### Gratitude Is the Foundation of The Law of Attraction

**WHEN YOU ARE GRATEFUL,** it's easier to maintain a positive attitude throughout your day. Even if it may be for just one aspect of your life, gratefulness gets you to focus on the good stuff.

Who doesn't appreciate gratitude and appreciation? Think about that for a minute. When you thank a person from your heart, when it is authentic gratitude, people are drawn to you. Gratitude is the foundation of the Law of Attraction.

What if you could create an environment where you are grateful for many other aspects of your life? Sometimes, it's simply thanking someone for doing something that you may have taken for granted up to this moment.

If your spouse does your laundry and you haven't thanked him or her lately, do so. Try being grateful for people who are in your life each and every day. It may take them by surprise when you thank them for this, but you'll find they will truly and sincerely appreciate your gratitude.

## The Law of Attraction Takes Commitment

Thoughts are an important part of the Law of Attraction. But, having one or two occasional thoughts on what you want out of life, isn't going to make much of a difference. You may get lucky, occasionally. Overall, however, you need to do more.

It's about committing yourself to the task. Learn the steps and then apply them. And although the steps are simple, it requires that you believe they work. Remember the 4-step process I talked about in chapter two? Refer to the ACTION NOTES at the end of the chapter for a quick refresh.

## The Difference Between The Law of Attraction and Goal Setting

Many people mistake the Law of Attraction with goal setting. In some cases, there are similarities between the two.

People don't always get goals right. Of course, people don't always get the Law of Attraction right.

However, when you figure out how to use the Law of Attraction, it will work. Some strive for goals that bring them down the wrong path. This is not to say that you can't use the Law of Attraction to help you achieve your goals.

Why people get them confused? Here's a predicament where the Law of Attraction may seem as not responding in one's favor. If you set goals that are not right for you, or if your goals are too aggressive, chances are you will get stressed by the intensity of the effort or disappointed by not being able to accomplish those goals.

When you create a plan (your goals), focus on the positive aspect of the plan and how it can get you to where you want to be in life. In this way, goals can be looked at as the path you set and the Law of Attraction as the power or the engine that will get you there.

## Can You Overuse The Law of Attraction?

The Law of Attraction is the energetic force that helps turn our dreams into reality. For those believers, is it possible to overuse this ability for selfish gain?

We all have wants and needs, and the very nature of the Law of Attraction allows us to obtain them. But, can we use the Law of Attraction in malicious ways that cause other people physical, emotional, or material harm?

Many believers of the Law of Attraction would reject this notion because it goes against what the concept is about. In other words, if you use it for ill intent, you set yourself up for negative consequences as a result.

This is why negative people often feel stuck in life. They aren't putting out positive vibes. Based on the basis of the theory one cannot overuse the Law of Attraction. In fact, one ought to embrace it in its fullest form to receive the most benefits from it.

When you use it for the positive intended purposes and for the highest good of all, what you receive in return will be creative energy that helps yourself and, in many cases, others as well. Embrace it and allow yourself to receive the benefits.

81 THE LAW OF **ATTRACTION**

Desire is the starting point of all achievement, not a hope, not a wish, but a keen pulsating desire which transcends everything.
Napoleon Hill

# VISUALIZATION:
## What Is Visualization?

**VISUALIZATION IS A GIFT** we've all been given and it is powerful. In simple terms, it is as the name implies. You create visual images in your mind. This in return activates the Law of Attraction bringing into your life the people, resources, events and circumstances as requested.

We think in terms of positive and negative imagery. If it were as simple as getting whatever our thoughts show, we would get some not so good things as well as the good. And it is true that people who focus primarily on the negative tend to draw more negativity into their lives. The truth is it takes more than random thoughts to make it work.

Visualization techniques help set your mind to create clear images of your IDEAL outcome. As you continue to focus on those images, it is easier to become creative generating new ideas to make your dreams come true.

While this sounds like a strange concept, it is not new. It has been around since the late 19$^{th}$ century, and some believe even earlier than that.

### Visualization: It's In the Script

Humans are visual beings. We constantly visualize images. We have an inner voice as well. But even when we speak words to ourselves, we are likely translating those to mental pictures.

So, it should come as no surprise to state that visualization is a strong concept in the toolbox of the Law of Attraction. But, with all the thousands of images that we hold in our brain daily, how do we focus on visualizations that will help us?

We can use scripts. These scripts will allow us to home in on the correct visualizations. When done right, we can set ourselves up to think creatively, as well as filter out any negative thoughts. When looked upon in this way, the more positive images you imagine, the less room there is for negative ones. There are, after all, only so many hours in a day.

Scripts are effective because they help paint the mental image for you, but it is up to you to practice them on a regular basis.

## Ways to Ace Visualization

It's a common misconception when dealing with visualization to believe that just by thinking of great images great things will happen. It's important to learn how to weed through the random images as we go through our day. Here's some ideas to help you get started:

**Pray or Meditate:** The practice of prayer and meditation relaxes the mind. It puts us into a state where we can perform our visualizations the best way possible. Create a ritual of daily meditation followed by visualizing your IDEAL outcome. See it as though it has already happened.

**Believe it is Possible:** Believing that through the Law of Attraction you can bring about the changes you need will give you a solid foundation to start building your dreams.

**Read "Your Invisible Power":** Many people believe that the power of visualization is a relatively new concept. But, as you can see when you read "Your Invisible Power" published in 1921, by Genevieve Behrend, this resource is almost 100 years old.

## Can You Use Visualization to Help Others?

There is much written on the power of the Law of Attraction and on using visualization to bring forth a better life.

It's a great tool for those who believe in it and who use it to improve themselves. But, is it possible to use the same techniques to help others?

If you are a proponent of the Law of Attraction, then you already know that you can take command of your own destiny by declaring your will to the universe.

Since we are all part of that universe, and we are interconnected via a cosmic channel of sorts, then we should by extension, be able to help others.

If you are skilled at using visualization, and there are specific techniques that you need to apply, then you have the ability to help others.

If someone is having difficulty finding work, why not visualize how you see them in a new job or career? You will find plenty of examples of people who swear this really works.

## Undisclosed Secrets Yet to Be Discovered

The world is like a giant puzzle, waiting for us to put the pieces together.

We can fly (airplanes) where this was unimaginable even 150 years ago. People thought it was impossible to go past 30 miles per hour when trains first emerged onto the scene. And yet, here we are in the 21st century with trains that can travel over 100 miles per hour.

We are given clues in the form of beliefs. What this means is that when we believe something is possible, i.e., when we can visualize something, we can make it happen.

The world, and by extension, the universe, wants us to make discoveries, for the benefit of the world. Imagine where we would be if we had no limiting beliefs throughout history. What about your own beliefs?

Do you hold any beliefs in things that may be impossible? What if you were to revisit them and choose to believe they are possible?

If you do, visualize what those impossibilities would be and you may even find a way to make them a reality. Use powerful affirmations to boost your visualizations.

# AFFIRMATIONS
# What Are Affirmations In The Law of Attraction?

The Law of Attraction allows us to take control of our lives by demanding of the Universe that certain things happen.

We tell the Universe what we want, and it responds by delivering. Those demands should be positive as negative demands will deliver negative results.

It's not enough, however, just to demand something once and expect things to happen. It takes believing in asking and receiving and reinforcing those beliefs. It's through using affirmations that you can continue to strengthen the bonds of the Law of Attraction.

Affirming sets the stage to receive the benefits of what it's being asked to be delivered.

## A Word Of Caution: Affirmations Will Only Work If You Are Willing to Change

*If you want to make affirmations work,* you will need to open to receiving the changes you desire. This seems so fundamental, and yet, many miss this point.

I've seen people give up way too soon. If they use an affirmation and don't see results right away, they pass them off as not working, or it wasn't meant to be. Remember this, instant gratification is not real and if it's meant to be, you make it to be.

Other times, even when affirmations do start to work, some people become fearful of the change that is taking place. Stepping out of our comfort zone can feel challenging because it means that we must change our thoughts and therefore perceptions. I know this feels like a stretch and it is.

The process of change can feel threatening for many of us but I have come to know it as the process of stepping into a better, greater version of ourselves.

*If you want to make affirmations work.* Another situation that arises is when speaking about your changes or affirmations to others. They may pass them off as superstition or have other misgivings about the practice.

If you can get past the doubters and even your own self-doubt, you will be well on your way to having something wonderful happen to you. Plus, you will set the stage to have many other wonderful things happen in your life.

## Did You Know Affirmations Can Help Your Love Life?

Many people believe in fate but is there more to love than this? It could be that using affirmations are the key to finding the right person for you.

Maybe you have experienced the situation where someone special came into your life after you giving up your quest for love. Could it be that you were using affirmations without even knowing that you were?

Try to think about the days or weeks before that happened. What thoughts were you thinking during that time?

Maybe you were thinking about what qualities you would like in a future mate.

Did you tell yourself you like someone who is tall or someone who is successful? Or, was the conversation with your mind about a person who is down-to-earth?

These are all aspects that you may have been focusing on during that time, and even though you eventually gave up, the Universe delivered for you.

It's likely that you were using affirmations. Give it a try. You just may find the right person by simply thinking about them.

## Is Your Inner-Critic Steering You Wrong?

You may believe in the power of affirmations, but how do they get squelched by your inner-critic?

These affirmations seem like a great idea, and several experts will say they work. But, if they do work, why aren't more people using them?

It could be that your inner-critic is stronger than any affirmations you may present for yourself. After all, we've spent a lifetime developing that critic. A few short-term affirmations aren't going to hold much weight against it.

It's going to take some work, but it can be done. It is about switching up your routine to use affirmations you find or create. If you are stuck finding the right affirmations, ask others who have found ones that work.

Repetition and belief are two important concepts when applying your affirmations. Set up a schedule that gives you the opportunity to practice your affirmation daily. Say your affirmations out loud several times throughout your day.

The more often you repeat your affirmations, the quicker you will transform your thinking style to the point where affirming becomes natural as the judging of the inner critic dissipates. Give it a try!

### Read Much About The Subject

There are many resources on the subject of the Law of Attraction. I encourage you to start learning and answering all the questions you will have after reading this simple introduction to such a complex matter.

Check out the short list of books I am including in the Acquiring Knowledge, section at the end of this booklet. These are books that helped me better understand how the Law of Attraction works.

Want to learn more about the incredible power of your mind? Read **"Imagine: The basics of Creative Visualization"**, in the Stella Notes Series, designed to help you tap into the power of your creative visualization and learn how to take your visualization skills to the next level.

# To acquire love,
# fill yourself up with it
# until you become a magnet.
### Charles Haanel

# ACT IV:

# Happiness Builders

# Tools-To-Use

92 STELLA FRANCES

## « Chapter Nine »

## PAY IT FORWARD

The principle of paying it forward was first recorded as early as 317 BC in ancient Greece from a play by Menander known as The Grouch. Benjamin Franklin referenced this concept in 1784, describing how we did not bestow upon someone a good deed but merely lent it to them so that they could give it to someone else in need later on. The naturalist and thinker Ralph Waldo Emerson eluded to this notion many times in his writings, as well.

While the sentiment has been noted many times throughout history, the phrase "pay it forward" did not appear in literature until 1916 when Lily Hardy Hammond wrote it in the book "In the Garden of Delight: "You don't pay love back;

you pay it forward." Later, this phrase and the ideals it represents appeared in everything from college sports to the guiding philosophy of Alcoholics Anonymous. Many charitable and humanitarian organizations espouse this same philosophy in their missions and guiding principles.

## Why is Paying it Forward So Powerful?

What exactly is the point of paying it forward? Why has this movement sparked so many projects and acts of generosity around the globe? There are actually some scientific studies that can help us understand the real power behind paying it forward.

It has long been known that performing good deeds makes you happier. Recent research at Stanford University sought to examine this phenomenon even further (Lyubomirsky, 2015). Participants were asked to perform at least five random acts of kindness each week for six weeks. Those in the study were allowed to pick the nature of their bestowed acts and when they wanted to engage in them.

When compared to the control group, who was not required to perform any good deeds, those who performed kind acts reported increased levels of happiness. Those who bestowed all of their weekly required acts in one single day showed the highest level of satisfaction after the study period ended.

What is it about giving to others that enhances your happiness? This question has a complicated answer, but the largest benefit of helping others is that it increases your sense of purpose in life. When you feel that your actions are directly responsible for improving someone else's life, you feel that you are having a positive influence on the world.

Acts of kindness provide you with a sense of control over your life and the world, too. Paying it forward is a way to enact the change that you would like to see in the world.

What happens when someone is so appreciative of your good deeds that they want to repay your generosity? You could accept their offer, or you could simply encourage the receiver to pay it forward. Honoring your kindness by bestowing a kind act on someone else is the foundation of paying it forward, and this represents an opportunity to show someone else how powerful good deeds can really be.

# WE LIFT OURSELVES UP BY HELPING OTHERS

## Helping Others Connect with The Law of Attraction

WHAT HAPPENS AFTER YOU DISCOVER the Law of Attraction works? You learn about how it works and then apply it to your own life. All of a sudden, your dreams are being realized, and you are living a happier lifestyle.

Whatever positive influences you obtained from the Law of Attraction, you now believe it works. If this is true, why not help others achieve the same? You could set out to help your family, friends and neighbors achieve a better life.

Of course, not everyone is going to be receptive to the idea of the Law of Attraction, but you will find the people who are open to the idea. These are the people who want to see positive changes in their lives and they are the ones you can help the most.

The positive effects of helping people will be returned to you in abundance. The satisfaction of helping others will be rewarded. If you found value in learning about the Law of Attraction in this book. If it helped you shift your mindset in any way, consider perhaps giving a copy to the people you love and care for their happiness and success in life.

# YOU CAN MAKE A DIFFERENCE
## My Favorite Story
## "The Starfish"

**ONE SUMMER'S MORNING** a little girl was walking on a long, winding beach. She came across a starfish that had been washed ashore and was now wriggling, and drying up in the hot sun. She reached down, gently picked up the starfish by one of its five points, and tossed it back to the sea. The little girl smiled and continued walking along the beach. But after a few steps, she found another starfish. It too was dying in the sun. No sooner had she tossed this one back when she came across another starfish, and then another one. Each time she found one, she picked it up and tossed it back to the sea.

She reached the top of a sand dune and came to a sudden stop. What she saw below startled and amazed her. Stretching out in front of her were hundreds upon hundreds, maybe even thousands, of dying starfish washed up on the beach. Suddenly, she exploded into action and began to toss as many starfish as possible, one by one, back to the sea.

She was so busy tossing back the starfish, that she never even noticed that a person had stopped to watch her. Soon a small crowd had gathered. Some started pointing at the little girl and laughing. *"That little girl's crazy,"* said one. *"I know,"* said another, *"doesn't she know that every summer thousands of starfish get washed up on the beach and die? It's just the way things are. There are so many starfish. She can't possibly make any difference."*

The little girl was still too busy tossing back starfish to notice them. Finally, one man decided he had seen enough. He walked over to the little girl. *"Little girl,"* he said, *"There are thousands of starfish washed up on the beach. You can't possibly hope, to make any real difference. Why don't you give up, and go play on the beach with the other children?"* The little girl's smile suddenly vanished. She noticed the crowd of people for the first time, and she realized they had been laughing at her. And now they had fallen silent, awaiting her answer to the man's question.

She was hot. She was tired, and close to tears. She began to think that maybe he was right. Maybe they were all right. She had been tossing back starfish for what seemed like hours, and yet a carpet of starfish still covered the beach. How could she have possibly thought she could make a difference? Her arms fell limp at her sides, and the starfish she was holding fell back to the hot sand. She started to walk away.

Then suddenly she stopped, turned around, reached back down, and picked up the starfish she had dropped. She swung back her arm and tossed the starfish as far as she possibly could. When it landed with a plop, she turned to the man, and with a huge smile on her face she said...

*"I made a difference to that one!"*

Inspired, a little boy emerged from the crowd, and he too picked up a starfish and sent it soaring back to the sea.

*"And I made a difference to that one!"* he said.

One by one every person in the crowd, old and young, joined in sending dying starfish back to the sea, calling, *"I made a difference to that one"* with each toss.

After a while the voices began to quiet down. The little girl became aware of this, and she wondered if the people were getting tired or discouraged. And so she looked across the beach. What she saw startled and amazed her. All the starfish were gone!

Many years later, another little girl was walking down the same beach. She reached the top of a sand dune, and came to a sudden stop. As far as her eyes could see, there were people tossing starfish into the sea. Curious, she approached an older man. *"Could you please tell me sir, why is everyone tossing starfish back into the sea?"*

The man, many years earlier, had been the little boy who was the first one to step forward and help the little girl save the starfish.

*"Little girl,"* he replied, *"each year, when a summer storm washes thousands of starfish onto the beach, the entire town comes out to toss them all back to the sea. You see, we learned one summer, many years ago, that when we all work together, we can actually make a huge difference."*

The Starfish Story – Adapted from 'The Star Thrower' by Loren C. Eiseley 1907 – 1977 (Eiseley, 1969)

The whole world can benefit in ways we may never even know, when we decide to make a difference in our world.

## Simple Ways to Pay it Forward

Here are 11 simple ways you can pay it forward today. What "pay it forward" ways can you think of?

Say something complimentary to the first five people you see today. But only if you really feel it and mean it. It must be a genuine, and heartfelt compliment.

Pay the toll for the driver behind you on the road.

Write an unsolicited recommendation for a colleague or coworker. Give it to your supervisor.

Deliver flowers to the nurse's station at your local hospital or nursing home, along with a note of thanks.

Leave a large tip for a service worker who has performed exceptionally well.

Smile at everyone you meet today.

Put coins into parking meters that are about to expire.

Organize a clean-up day at your local park, or beach.

Leave an inspirational note on the mirror of a public bathroom to help the next person feel special or loved.

Buy coffee for the person behind you in the drive-through line.

Make a list of all the things you love and appreciate about your partner and give it to them.

What "pay it forward" ways can you think of?

## ELEVATE YOUR HAPPINESS

*Many people die with their music still in them. Why is this so? Too often it is because they are always getting ready to live. Before they know it, time runs out.*
OLIVER W. HOLMES

**JUST THE OTHER DAY,** I came across the above quote and I am sharing it with you because it hit a chord in my heart. It helped me become even more aware about first, *what do I do with the song in my heart?* Second, *how do I help others step into their power to express their music?* That sweet song that's waiting patiently in everyone's heart to be sung.

We've all been blessed with special gifts and talents unique to each one of us. For some of us, for various reasons and life experiences, it takes a little more to build or rebuild self-esteem and acknowledge our uniqueness. I know this concept well, I've been there a few times myself. Have you ever felt like you don't fit because you are so different? There was a time when I used to believe that I was a misfit

Truth is. We don't fit because we are not supposed to fit. Each one of us is uniquely created not intended to fit in a one-size fits all box. No Way! Yet, some of us, spend years of our lives trying to fit until one day we finally realize we definitely don't fit. That's when we might do something even worst than trying to fit in the one-size fits all box.

We build our own box and lock ourselves in it. We close down. We give up on us and we let life take us wherever life wants to take us. We give away our right to create, to produce, to be happy, peaceful, and successful. As time goes by, we don't see our gifts anymore. We blind ourselves with the darkness of the box we've built for us. And what is that special gift, only you carry in your heart? What is the uniqueness you run away from?

Get the picture? This maybe you, or maybe someone you know. A long time ago, that was definitely me. That's what my before looked like.

I changed my before and I love my after. My after I am now living, as I am writing this for you. How about you? How would you like to step out of your before and into your after? Making your now extraordinary. Make it match You. Your fantastic unique and extraordinary gifts. Learn to express your music. Learn to live up to your potential.

Are you ready? Step up to your next level of being. You have tremendous potential. Take right action and put it to work for you. You've got this!

What makes you unique? I encourage you to discover and learn to express your uniqueness. Sing the song in your heart. I so believe in the power of your spirit.

# STRATEGY NOTES

## Pay It Forward

- ✓ Say something complimentary to the first five people you see today. But only if you really feel it and mean it. It must be a genuine, and heartfelt compliment.
- ✓ Pay the toll for the driver behind you on the road.
- ✓ Write an unsolicited recommendation for a colleague or coworker. Give it to your supervisor.
- ✓ Deliver flowers to the nurse's station at your local hospital or nursing home, along with a note of thanks.
- ✓ Leave a large tip for a service worker who has performed exceptionally well.
- ✓ Smile at everyone you meet today.
- ✓ Put coins into parking meters that are about to expire.
- ✓ Organize a clean-up day at your local park, or beach.
- ✓ Leave an inspirational note on the mirror of a public bathroom to help the next person feel special or loved.
- ✓ Buy coffee for the person behind you in the drive-through line.
- ✓ Make a list of all the things you love and appreciate about your partner and give it to them.

104 STELLA FRANCES

# Words Of Wisdom

wise words spoken by some of
the most powerful and
advanced thinkers in our
world. Listen to the
echo of their voices
and use their wisdom in
your moment-to-moment life.

# WORDS OF WISDOM

# Attitude Is A Little Thing That Makes A Big Difference.
## Winston Churchill

## WORDS OF WISDOM

Richness is not about what you have. It is about who you are.
Bob Proctor

## WORDS OF WISDOM

Optimism is the faith that leads to achievement. Nothing can be done without hope or confidence.
Hellen Keller

## WORDS OF WISDOM

# The size of your success is determined by the size of your belief.
David Schwartz

110 STELLA FRANCES

# Pearls Of Kindness

inspire and motivate yourself to thrive on your path to happiness and success

# POWERFUL AFFIRMATIONS

## I Have Wealth And Abundance.

Wealth and abundance are all around me. I can easily see the opportunities in my life that allow for abundance. *My inner voice tells me of these opportunities; all I have to do is listen to it.*

When I have time for myself, I repeat positive affirmations about wealth and abundance. This helps to keep positive thoughts and images in my mind. *I am a receiver of great things.* The power of the Creator provides for all of my needs.

When I first wake up in the morning, I give thanks for all that I have. I know that being grateful is the first step to receiving more. The world has endless wealth; there is enough for everyone.

Whenever I feel challenged by my bills, I take a deep breath and relax. I remind myself that the world is full of money and much is earmarked for me.

*At night, my final thoughts before sleep are about wealth and abundance.* I smile knowing that great wealth is coming to me. I sleep deeply and soundly every night.

Today, I am grateful that I have wealth and abundance and know I can attract even more. The opportunities all around me are just waiting for me to grab hold of them.

**Self-Reflection Questions**

How does it make me feel when I imagine having great wealth?

What signs of wealth and abundance are in my life?

Can I use my wealth and abundance to help others? Who? How?

Voice your thoughts here…

_____
_____
_____
_____
_____
_____
_____
_____
_____
_____

## POWERFUL AFFIRMATIONS

I can and I will.
End of story.

I am adventurous. I overcome fears by following my dreams.

I am not a product of my circumstances. I am a product of my decisions.

I am rich in relationships, wealth, and love.

## SOULFUL REFLECTIONS

### I Give Love Without Question.

It is in my nature to extend positive energy to those around me. *Love is in abundance within my soul so I give it without question.*

I believe that even the simplest gestures go a long way. Saying good morning to strangers allows an exchange of good vibes. I am conscious of the positive impact it has so I do it whenever I am able.

When a friend misses out on an opportunity, my first instinct is to offer comfort. I recognize when someone yearns for quiet love and caring without judgmental statements. I understand emotions and seek to reenergize the healthy feelings.

*Anyone who comes to me for a kind word, prayer, or a helping hand receives it.*

My life is fulfilling because I am able to share light and joy with others. I grow more compassionate when I give love unconditionally.

Today, there is more love within me than I am able to keep to myself. I look out for opportunities to share it and make the lives of others happier. My commitment to extending positivity to the world is unwavering.

116 STELLA FRANCES

# Relaxing Mandalas

## Express Your Inner-Artist

beautiful mandalas to help you find inner peace by being in the moment

You can use color pencils or just your regular pen, markers are not recommended as the ink may bleed through the paper.

## RELAXING MANDALAS

# RELAXING MANDALAS

These days many of us feel overworked and overwhelmed. Our modern lives are faster-paced than ever, and often feel as though they're spinning out of control. Luckily, the mandala appears to us as a reminder to relax and rejuvenate.

The word Mandala (pronunciation mon- dah- lah) means "circle" and represents the universe in Indian religions. The mandala appears to us in all aspects of life. It encompasses friends, family, and communities.

Life is circular. Life is never-ending. Each moment is another colorful thread in the continually growing tapestry of the universe.

The ritual of mandala coloring moves us into a contemplative state, encouraging us to slow down.

Allow your stress to melt away as you enter the world of circles and patterns. Become one with the Universe as you lose yourself to the flow of lines and color.

Allow yourself to move from the doing to the being as you enjoy the process of transformative ritual!

# RELAXING MANDALAS

121 THE LAW OF **ATTRACTION**

# RELAXING MANDALAS

# YOUR NOTES: TOOLS-TO-USE

## TOOLS-TO-USE

1. Love & Kindness: Pay it forward
2. Visualization: See it. Believe it
3. Affirmations: Affirm it
4. Mandalas: Doodle your way into Focusing, Meditating and Inner Peace

Take action today. Choose one or all of the above easy to use tools and start enjoying the benefits of being happier and at peace right away.

# IN CLOSING:

## BONUS MATERIAL

Two Gifts For You

# Gift #1: Heartfelt Affirmations For You To Thrive On Your Path To Happiness

*Each new day brings me an opportunity to work towards my biggest goals. I am blessed with the benefit of planning my life.*

*It is important to me to make the most of what I have. When I avoid taking things for granted, I maintain a sense of appreciation.*

*Gratitude for my blessings encourages me to take a path of charity. It helps me to focus on the needs of others as a way of achieving personal fulfillment.*

*When my help has an impact on others, I am persuaded to continue along the trajectory of kindness.*

*I spend time on the path of hard work because the results are impactful. I enjoy the feeling of accomplishment I get when my effort produces great things.*

*Each thing I achieve as a result of hard work pushes me to keep working. I know that sincere and honest efforts are important for me to achieve specific targets.*

*Fear rarely gets in the way of my steps when I commit to giving everything my best effort.*

*Today, I use every opportunity to develop a life of gratitude, kindness, and perseverance.*

*I am committed to building the most successful life possible. However, my steps in life are preceded by the desire to be my best self.*

# Gift #2: Golden Tips for Your Overall Well Being

I've saved the best for last. These super uplifting and furiously fun self-development golden tips are for you and you alone.

**Laugh out loud-** laugh until your cheeks hurt, laugh until your stomach aches, and laugh until the tears are rolling down your face. You've heard it before; laughter is the best medicine.

*Set daily goals-* self-improvement comes from within which is why you need to work towards setting your own goals each day. This could be work related, diet related or anything else related. Start small and always reward yourself for meeting the challenges of your daily goals. Missed a goal? Don't beat yourself up, as long as you don't quit, it will be alright. Start again tomorrow.

*Face you fears-* are you afraid of heights? Go skydiving. This is one of the most liberating things you can do. Are you afraid of speaking in public? Find a small group and deliver a short speech on a subject you have mastered. When you look your fear in the eye and go for it, fear disappears

*Travel to a foreign place-* seeing the sights of a different culture is a great pleasure in life. Not only will it open your mind to new things, but it will also enhance your love for home and increase your sense of what's important. Travelling is one the best ways to find yourself, especially when you chose to travel independently.

***Have Fun*-** life is not always about work. You need to find that balance. Try to schedule something that you love to do for at least once a month. This could involve drinks with friends, camping with family or simply indulging in a day of "you". Bring Sunday back and make it Lazy-Sunday.

***Dress up*** once and a while- okay, so prom was ages ago, but this does not mean you cannot doll yourself up once in a while. Putting on a beautiful gown or tuxedo and spending money on new shoes and a new haircut can make you feel like a Princess, or a Prince. And every person deserves to feel special once and a while.

***Express your Love*-** tell your Mom you love her; call up a friend and let her know she's the best, for no reason at all. Showing others how much you mean to them will help you realize how important they really are, and how lucky you are to have them in your life. Knowing that they feel the same about you can truly boost your self-confidence and importance.

***Make time for Hobbies*-** it's important for people to have hobbies. As we get older it's easy to stop those extra-curricular activities that you loved as a child such as sports. Look for adult activities such as soccer teams, book clubs, rowing clubs or bird watching groups. Keep your passions alive by re-connecting with the hobbies and activities that you once loved.

***Look down*-** take a hike to the top of a cliff that overlooks the city or jump on an elevator and ride the lift to the top floor and look down. Seeing the world from this above can really put things into a new perspective.

*Break the Pattern*- get up, work, home, gym, dinner, TV, sleep. Does this sound like your pattern to life, or something similar? Break it up.

*Find a Balance*- it's all about harmony. Finding that perfect balance comes down to mind, body and spirit. Work on perfecting all three to gain self-importance.

*Live for the Now*- sure, you need to plan for the future, but live for the moment! This can be a little tricky, but the key is to find that balance between saving for tomorrow and living for today. Opt for a savings account for the future and keep a special account for the Now, just in case you see a beautiful dress on sale, or you and your buddies decide to rush off to the islands for the weekend.

*Learn something new*- knowledge is power. Whether this is learning a new language, just for the sake of it, learning how to cook, or learning how to make pottery, you are never too old to learn. Learning will keep your mind active and helps improve your sense of self-worth.

*Dance like there's no one watching*- this may seem like an odd choice to end our ever-important Law of Attraction reading but, in a sense, it's the most important tip.

This is because, in order to really get what you want in life you have to find your self-worth and truly love your life, you need to feel it from the inside. You need to let go of all the stresses and judgements of your surroundings including your finances, your family, your relationships and your career.

So, put on your favorite song and release all of insecurities by jiving around your living room.

- ❖ Dance away those work dramas.
- ❖ Dance away those relationship issues.
- ❖ Dance away those money woes.
- ❖ Dance your way to self-improvement.

The way to personal excellence and true happiness is a long journey that sometimes may feel like an uphill battle both ways. Why walk through the bumps and jolts when you can dance?

So, my last golden tip comes from the advice of David Bowie: *Just Dance!*

The rest will fall into place.

130 STELLA FRANCES

# AFTERWORD

resource guide for living a better, happier purpose-driven life

## A Note From Stella Frances

If you've made it this far, then I can tell we are going to be friends. You - like me - are always exploring how you can grow and be your best-self. I'm inspired by people like you and would love to embrace you as part of the tribe.

To learn more about how to *"Find Your Happy"* by creating a meaningful and purpose driven life visit StellaFrances.com or come to a private workshop or mini-retreat where we can meet in person and we can dig into Careers & Relationships over soulful conversations. For a list of upcoming events remember to go to: StellaFrances.com/events/

I'd love to connect with you and hear about your journey. So be sure to stay in touch. Feel free to send me a quick note or say hello on Facebook and keep me posted. I'm here to help!

Here's to leading a life of purpose and living with passion!

*Stella xo*

PS  Visit the blog StellaFrances.com/blog page for daily inspiration and tips on creating the life you love living. I can help you succeed in your pursuit of happiness.

PPS  As, Zig Ziglar once said... *"People often say that motivation doesn't last. Well, neither does bathing, that's why we recommend it daily"*

# A SPECIAL INVITATION
# Find Your Happy Discovery Call

## Set up An Exclusive Appointment with A Whole New Level Of Happiness.

*Are you ready to move your happiness up to a new level?*

**Explore and Discover What Really Matters To You.** I invite you to a complimentary call with me to explore and discover the ways to bring more happiness into your life.

We all experience the ups and downs of life and I'm here to help keep you going in the right direction, just because we all deserve to be happy!

A "Find-Your-Happy" Discovery Session is a 30-minute call. where we talk about where in life you are now and where you'd love to be.

Specifically, here's what we will cover during our call:

### The 3 D's:

1. *Discover* the longing and discontent in the areas of your life you'd like to improve and what is costing you to stay where you are. That would be our first step.

2. *Design* a clear vision for the quality of life you desire and what's worth to take happiness to the next level. That would be our second step.

3.     *Decide* to take today the action that will move you from where you are to where you want to be. That would be the third step in taking your Happiness to a higher level.

Leave this session feeling uplifted and inspired knowing that you have the power to change your life and that the power within you is far greater than your current life conditions and circumstances.

Right now, you're standing at the doorway to your new ideal life. Get clear on exactly where you are, what you'd like to create, and the next most important step you can take that will move you in the direction of a happier-purpose driven life.

Join me for a complimentary 30-min. discovery call. Every week I make sure I carve out a chunk of time to offer free service to community. This is my way to say thank you and "pay-it-forward." As you can imaging spots are limited. To schedule your session, jump over to the website and let's talk soon! To access my calendar, go to StellaFrances.com/calendar/

I'm here to help!

## YOUR NEXT BEST STEP
## Need More In-Depth Guidance Creating A Happiness Based Life?

### These will help...

We have created some incredibly in-depth programs, courses and products to help you every step of the way on your pursuit of happiness. And as with everything we do at Elevated Awareness, they come with a 100% results-backed guarantee. That's just how confident I am they work.

### Two great places to start are:

### An Empowering Self-Discovery Adventure

# Find Your Happy

Find it and Claim it! Know who you are and be who you are! With this step-by-step framework Stella helps her clients take time to find themselves, understand what they want in their lives, and take effective right action to make their dreams come true. This program is for you if you want to bring more happiness and success into your life by finding meaning, purpose and direction.

Happiness fuels success; **if you want to be more successful, be happier!** Stella's coaching will empower you to achieve your goals whilst simultaneously increasing your happiness. Take action and begin your pursuit of true happiness, today.

# A Journey Into Life Mastery

# THE PASSPORT

*Passport to your dream.* If you are ready for a new destination. If it feels like something is missing where you are in your life right now, get ready to DEFINE your IDEAL outcome and DECIDE to go after it.

If you're willing to commit to your happiness and ready to take action to change your life, then you have found the program that will help you move forward.

THE PASSPORT is a step-by-step proven system that helps you get crystal clear on what you want and gives you the tools and strategies to stay true to yourself. Learn the simple steps that will take you from wherever you are now (stuck, frustrated, scared, unhappy) to confident and fulfilled as you learn exactly how to define your dream and develop a concrete plan to achieve it.

When you are in harmony with your soul's purpose and with what you are here to be and do, things get easier. This is the most passionate, wondrous way to live life. Sign up and start living the life you were meant to live.

**VIP Day** Every intensive is unique. You may choose to come work with me in person, or virtually from the comfort of your own home or office. Join me for jam-packed self-discovery action over the course of a fun filled day.

# STELLA NOTES & CLUB ★ HAPPY

## Solutions From The Soul

Winning ways to play the game of life. Check out this popular mini guide series on finding true lasting happiness and take your life to the next level. Stella Notes are short writings super loaded with practical tools, easy-to-use strategies, and pearls of wisdom to help you uncover your passions, remove roadblocks and get you moving from where you are to where you want to be.

Imagine what it would feel like to belong to a group that combined the benefits of a social group, mastermind group, support group, cheerleader group. Imagine what it would feel like to create relationships with like-minded people who not only understand your thirst to discover your truth and make your dreams come true, but who also believe that you can achieve the goals you set for yourself.

These are just some of the benefits you will enjoy as a member of Club-Happy. Visit StellaFrances.com/clubhappy

Curious to know more? All of the courses, products and free resources to support you on your life journey can be found at: StellaFrances.com

Make your journey a fun one.

*"Success Begins with Happiness"*
STELLA FRANCES

# About Stella Frances

## Mentor, Coach, Speaker, Creator of Stella-Notes

Stella Frances, founder of Elevated Awareness, inspires and empowers all those that are drawn to her to live their highest vision in the context of love and joy.

As a Success Principles, Jack Canfield Certified Trainer and as a Mary Morrissey Certified DreamBuilder Coach, Stella can help you design and manifest a life that's in harmony with your soul's purpose.

After 15 successful years in the I.T. industry, Stella-Frances found herself more passionate in coaching her clients around systems for life than in I.T. systems. Her passion is teaching clients discover & unlock their unique potential, find true happiness and achieve success to live a life they LOVE living.

Stella is an inspiring speaker, passionate educator, and a highly sought-after happiness coach.

What is the biggest challenge you're facing right now? And what would you love to create? Let Stella help you, or your employees break through the obstacles that are holding you back. You will be glad you did.

To contact Stella, go to her website at StellaFrances.com

### Qualifications and Certifications

- Success Principles Trainer - Jack Canfield (Chicken Soup for the Soul)
- DreamBuilder Coach - Mary Morrissey, Transformational Coaching
- Access Bars™ Practitioner - Gary Douglas, Access Consciousness
- Langevin Certified Instructor/Facilitator

## Programs and Workshops

Stella Frances gives talks and leads workshops all over the United States and the Caribbean Islands.

She also conducts retreats, intensives, and training programs.

To learn more, go to StellaFrances.Com/Events

# Island Retreat with Stella Frances
# The Voyage

## ADVENTURES INTO HAPPINESS

The ticket to happiness is hidden in your heart. Get out of your day-to-day grind and jump into the source of true happiness and wellbeing. Connect with nature as you set your intentions to bring more happiness into your life.

Create a powerful vision of your IDEAL life, set goals and define effective action to make it happen. Learn how to change your thoughts to change your world.

If you'd like Stella's personal help in defining the framework and start building an exciting life based on your definition of happiness, these small-group private retreats held in exclusive locations like the quaint Bahamas, Jamaica, and Jupiter Beach offer a tranquil, transformational environment and personalized support you need to awaken to the best <u>You</u>.

Reject stress and give yourself the gift of time to attain inner-peace and a sense of empowerment. Get inspired with our sunrise meditation on the beach. Enjoy healthy delicious freshly cooked meals. Come home with an island mindset and a solid plan to maintain it, no matter how gray the sky gets.

**Recharge and Reboot At A Retreat By-The-Sea.**

For information and to reserve your spot, contact Stella at Happier@StellaFrances.com

## Bring The Power Of Change To Your Organization

# Steps to Success

### KEYNOTE, WORKSHOP, AND TRAINING

Positive change and profound success are the results when your employees and managers, experience **Steps to Success** in a live group workshop, training, or keynote.

Not only will your team be inspired and motivated to achieve greater success, but they'll also learn how to up-level all their mind-sets, actions, relationships, and strategic alliances.

**Steps to Success** Keynote, Workshop, or Training will empower them with strategies that make them more productive, help put more money in their paychecks, help them function better within their workgroups, and respond more effectively and productively to everyday events.

The **Steps to Success** *is ideal for groups such as:*
- Small-business owners
- Managers and executives
- Corporate workgroups and new hires
- Professional practitioners and their staffs
- Work-at-home employees and telecommuters
- Employees facing layoff or transfer

To learn more, go to StellaFrances.com or contact Stella at Happier@StellaFrances.com

## 90-Day Programs with Stella Frances

# The Passport

**Voyage into Happiness**

A Life Mastery Course of Action. Getting you from where you are to where you want to be.

# Find *Your* Happy

**A Self-Discovery & Empowerment Journey**

Bring more happiness into your life by finding meaning, purpose and direction.

## The Ticket
### You Were Born To Be Happy

**A 2-STEP FORMULA TO BRING MORE HAPPINESS & SUCCESS INTO YOUR PROFESSIONAL LIFE**

Step 1: Making your business more effective.

Step 2: Becoming a more effective *you*.

---

## The Dream Builder
### Journey into The Spirit
The Spiritual Laws of Success

Learn how everything is created twice — and how you can use that truth to build your dreams effortlessly.

**YOUR HAPPINESS COACH**
**GROUP. ONE-ON-ONE. VIP-DAY. RETREATS. WORKSHOPS**

## Weekend Workshops with Stella Frances

# THE MECHANICS OF LIFE
### Elevating Self-Awareness

### An Irresistibly Fun Series Of 5 Self-Growth Mix-&-Match Workshops

#1. Master the Mindset of Success.
#2. Goal Setting For Growth.
#3. Building Inner Confidence.
#4. The Power Of Saying No.
#5. Elevate Your Energy.

---

## The Vision
### Tailor Life to Your Dreams

Start actively pursuing the dream that will give you the joy, confidence and happiness you're longing for.

*To learn more, go to StellaFrances.com or contact Stella at Happier@StellaFrances.com*

*Stella Frances*
**YOUR HAPPINESS COACH**
**GROUP. ONE-ON-ONE. VIP-DAY. RETREATS. WORKSHOPS**

# Aquiring Knowledge And Additional Resources For Happiness And Success

I trust you enjoyed reading the *Stella-Notes* on the Law of Attraction and have found it both helpful and interesting. Above all I hope it piqued your curiosity enough to make you want to dive deeper and learn more.

While we've covered the core principles of the Law of Attraction, there's much more to learn and explore. I suggest and recommend that you read something educational and motivational every day, at least 15-minutes a day, or more.

Create a new ritual to inspire and motivate yourself. Keep reading, keep learning, and keep practicing as you work your way towards the life of your dreams. Happiness is attainable by each one of us. Make it happen!

**Knowledge is Power:** Curious To Learn More? Here's A Start…

Ask and It Is Given by Esther Hicks.
Your Invisible Power by Genevieve Behrend.
Think and Grow Rich by Napoleon Hill.

## Awesome Titles Available In The Stella Notes Series

- ❖ Imagine
- ❖ Dreams Come True
- ❖ Inspired
- ❖ Being Happier
- ❖ No Worries
- ❖ Stuck No More
- ❖ Happy by Habit
- ❖ Mindfully Yours

# Take Your Happiness To The Next Level... Download The FREE Happiness Tools

## At StellaFrances.com/resources

### Tool #1: Daily Gratitude Journal

Use the Gratitude Journal to record you wins and gifts of the day. It's an awesome self-discovery tool that can help you connect with your unique character strengths.

### Tool #2: Stuck? Unstick Yourself Now Worksheet

An easy tool to use for when you feel stuck or want to generate new ideas for a project or goal. This super-effective brainstorming tool helps you come up with lots of new ideas and choose 3 actions to move forward with.

### Tool #3: Stressed? Overwhelmed? Speedy Priority Finder

Sometimes your day-to-day priorities differ from your life's priorities. Use this tool to feel more in control and less overwhelmed. Clarify a path to set and realize top priorities.

### Tool #4: Daily Success Habits Exercise

By making small changes to your daily routine you can make BIG changes in your life and career. Define 5 new success habits, to help you be more effective.

### 5-DAY SELF-DISCOVERY COURSE

In this powerful FREE **Grow-Expand-Thrive** mini course -delivered to your email address- you will learn winning ways to find your happy and start living a more fulfilled and meaningful life. Register today at StellaFrances.com

www.ingramcontent.com/pod-product-compliance
Lightning Source LLC
Chambersburg PA
CBHW022104160426
43198CB00008B/350